Our Community Helpers

Farmers Help

by Dee Ready

Consulting Editor: Gail Saunders-Smith, PhD

CAPSTONE PRESS
a capstone imprint

Pebble Books are published by Capstone Press,
1710 Roe Crest Drive, North Mankato, Minnesota 56003
www.capstonepub.com

Library of Congress Cataloging-in-Publication Data
Ready, Dee.
  Farmers help / by Dee Ready.
      pages cm.—(Pebble Books. Our community helpers)
  Includes bibliographical references and index.
  Summary: "Simple text and full-color photographs describe a farmer's tools,
workplace, and role in the community"—Provided by publisher.
  Audience: Ages 6-8. Audience: Grades K-3.
  ISBN 978-1-4765-3951-5 (library binding)—ISBN 978-1-4765-5155-5 (pbk.)—
  ISBN 978-1-4765-6012-0 (ebook PDF)
  1. Farmers—Juvenile literature. I. Title. II. Series: Pebble. Our community helpers.
  S519.R43 2014
  636—dc23   2013030100

Editorial Credits
Erika L. Shores, editor; Gene Bentdahl, designer;
Charmaine Whitman, production specialist

Image Credits
Alamy: Tetra Images, LLC, 4; Capstone Studio: Karon Dubke, cover, 6, 8, 14, 16;
Getty Images: aquaArts studio, 20, Mayur Kakade, 10; Shutterstock: Alf Ribeiro, 14,
Goodluz, 12; SuperStock: FLPA, 18

Note to Parents and Teachers

The Our Community Helpers set supports national social studies
standards for how groups and institutions work to meet individual
needs. This book describes and illustrates farmers. The images
support early readers in understanding the text. The repetition of
words and phrases helps early readers learn new words. This book
also introduces early readers to subject-specific vocabulary words,
which are defined in the Glossary section. Early readers may need
assistance to read some words and to use the Table of Contents,
Glossary, Read More, Internet Sites, and Index sections of the book.

Printed in the United States   5978

Table of Contents

What Is a Farmer?

Farmers are people who grow and raise the food we eat. Farmers make sure crops grow and animals stay healthy.

What Farmers Do

Farmers work from sunrise to sunset. They feed farm animals. They plow the ground and plant seeds. Farmers fix machines and farm buildings.

Farms have many buildings.
Silos and bins hold grain.
Barns hold animals.
Farmers usually live in
a farmhouse on the farm.

The crops farmers grow depend on where they live. Vegetables grow best where it's warm year-round. Grains grow where summers are warm.

Livestock farmers raise animals for food to sell. Dairy farmers sell the milk from cows. Poultry farmers raise chickens for eggs and meat.

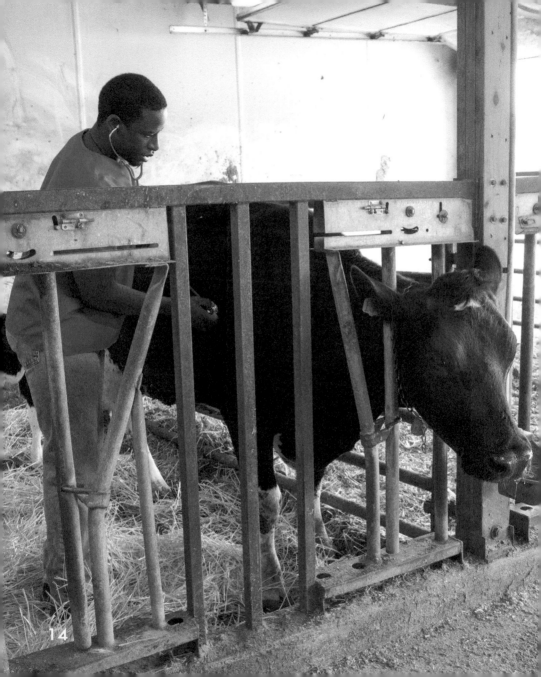

Farmers often work by themselves. Sometimes they help each other harvest crops. Veterinarians help farmers care for their animals.

Tools and Clothes

Farmers use many tools.
Tractors and combines help
plant and harvest crops.
Farmers use wrenches to
fix machines.

Farming is dangerous work. Gloves and boots protect hands and feet. Thick jeans protect a farmer's legs. A hat shades a farmer's eyes.

Farmers Help

Without farmers there would not be any food. Farmers help people in their communities. Farmers also help grow food for people around the world.

Glossary

combine—a large farm machine that is used to gather crops

community—a group of people who live in the same area

crop—a plant farmers grow in large amounts, usually for food; farmers grow crops such as corn, soybeans, and peas

grain—the seed of a cereal plant such as wheat, rice, corn, rye, or barley

harvest—to gather crops that are ready to pick and eat

tractor—a powerful motor vehicle with large rear wheels, used mainly on farms for pulling equipment and trailers

veterinarian—a doctor who treats sick or injured animals; veterinarians also help animals stay healthy

Read More

Arlon, Penelope, and Tory Gordon-Harris. *Farm.* Scholastic Discover More. New York: Scholastic, 2012.

Dickman, Nancy. *Jobs on a Farm.* World of Farming. Chicago: Heinemann Library, 2011.

Kawa, Katie. *My First Trip to the Farm.* My First Adventures. New York: Gareth Stevens Pub., 2013.

Internet Sites

FactHound offers a safe, fun way to find Internet sites related to this book. All of the sites on FactHound have been researched by our staff.

Here's all you do:

Visit *www.facthound.com*

Type in this code: 9781476539515

Check out projects, games and lots more at
www.capstonekids.com

Index

Word Count: 193
Grade: 1
Early-Intervention Level: 18